This edition first published 1998
by Hodder Children's Books
A Division of Hodder Headline plc
338 Euston Road
London NW1 3BH

A catalogue record for this book is available from
the British Library

ISBN 0 340 71666 5

Printed and bound in Great Britain
by The Devonshire Press Ltd., Torquay, Devon TQ2 7NX

# Postman Pat™
## and the
## Ice-ladder

John Cunliffe
Illustrated by Stuart Trotter

from the original television
designs by Ivor Wood

Hodder
Children's
Books

a division of Hodder Headline plc

For George,
and all beginners
J.C.

## Chapter One

# A hard winter

It was a hard winter in
Greendale. The roads were
blocked with deep snow.

1

Postman Pat had to wait for the snowplough to get through before he could deliver his letters.

There were frozen pipes all
over Greendale, and Ted was
kept busy mending them.

The children loved the snow!
They got their sledges out, and
pulled them to the top of a
snowy hill.

Then they went whizzing all
the way down to the bottom,
faster and faster.

There was a deep snowdrift at
the bottom, where the snow
was nice and soft.

Here they all tumbled off
their sledges, laughing and
shouting.

The snow gave them a soft and safe landing but it got inside their wellies and made their socks wet.

It soon soaked into their gloves, making their fingers sting. But never mind that!

They were soon off to the top
of the hill again, for another
whizzzzzzz down to the bottom.

They forgot wet hands and feet
in the excitement of the fast
run down the hill.

When it was time to go home, the mums and dads came out and shouted, "Katy and Tom! Time for bed! Come along, now!"

"Julian! Bedtime!"
But they never wanted to go home, cold as they might be. It was such wonderful fun in the snow.

It was getting quite dark. The
mums and dads waited at the
bottom of the hill, while the
children shouted,
"Just one more!
Please!" It was
once more, and
once more yet
again, until
the grown-ups
were tired of
waiting, and
dragged them
all home,
and off
to bed.

But first they had hot baths, and supper by a lovely warm fire before they cuddled up in cosy beds, with a bedtime story.

Then they went to sleep, and dreamed of another day of sledging, and all the fun that winter brings.

When they were not sledging,
they built snow houses, and
snowmen, and snow women,
and had snow battles.

"I wish winter would go on for
ever," said Julian.

# Chapter Two

# A brilliant place

The children sledged every day. Then, on Saturday, Katy said, "Let's find somewhere else to sledge. I'm tired of this hill." "All right," said Tom. "Where shall we go?"

"I know a place," said
Lucy Selby.
"Come on, then," said Julian.
"Show us!"
They trudged through the deep
snow, across two fields, and
along by the church.

Pat passed them in his van,
and gave them a wave.

On they went, until Lucy said,
"Here it is! This is a brilliant
place!"

They had forgotten what Mr
Pringle said on Tuesday
morning, in school.
"Whatever you do," he said,
"don't go on the ice on the
lake. It's very, very dangerous."
There, at the bottom of this
hill, was the lake, covered with
ice, shining in the winter sun.

## Chapter Three

# On the ice

They never meant to go on the
ice. After all, Mr. Pringle said,
"Don't go *on* the ice," he didn't
say, "Don't go *near* the ice."
So it seemed quite safe to
sledge in that field.

At least, that's what they all
thought, and they meant just
to sledge in the field.

But there was the ice so near,
and it looked so wonderful,
so smooth and clean. Off they
went up the hill, and down
they came – *whizzzzzzzzzzz*.
It was a wonderful place
to sledge.

All went well until someone (who *was* it?) found a part of the hill where they could go even faster. They went so fast that they couldn't stop, and they went out on to the ice.

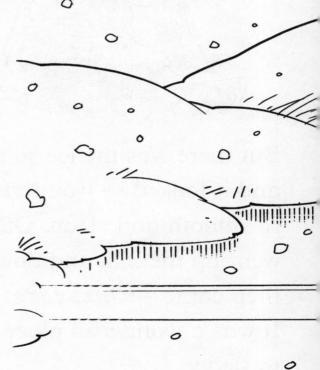

When they were on the ice, the sledges went faster still! And it seemed quite safe. The ice was as hard as rock! It must be safe.

So, the next time, they all went on to the ice. How exciting it was! It was the most wonderful sledging they had ever known.

Again and again, they went on
to the ice. . .

. . . and each time they went a
little bit further out.

Then, just when Katy and Tom
had gone down together on
one sledge, and gone skimming
far across the ice, there was a
loud crackling sound.

The ice split itself open,
between Katy and Tom and
the shore, and they could not
get back.

They were on an ice-boat,
floating on black water.

## Chapter Four

# Help!

Lucy and Julian stopped their
sledges at the edge of the
water. They could see Katy
and Tom, with their sledge,
bobbing about on the piece
of floating ice.

"Help!" shouted Lucy.

"Keep still!" shouted Julian, "or the ice will tip you in the water."

"Quick!" said Lucy. "Run and get my dad! He'll know what to do."

"It's too far to the village," said Julian, "but..."

He had just heard a sound he knew so well. It was the sound of an engine, a van's engine, Postman Pat's van, on its way with the post!

He would know it anywhere, that *chug-chug-splutter-chug-cough-bang-splutter-chug-chug* sound.

Oh! How wonderful it was to hear it just now! But they were hidden from the road by a high hedge. Pat might go past without seeing them!

Julian ran as he had never run before. He fairly flew across the snowy grass. He was at the gate in time, *just* in time, only just, to flag Pat down as he came slowly, carefully, round the slippery corner.

## Chapter Five

# A useful man

Pat stopped in the gateway,
and jumped out of the van.
"Dad, Dad!" panted Julian.
He was so out of breath that
he could not get the words out.

"Somebody on the ice?" said
Pat. "Is it Katy and Tom? I
heard that ice cracking half a
mile away. Right, now you
stay here and look after Lucy.

You must not, *not*, try to go on
the ice to rescue them. Just stay
in the field and you'll be okay.

I'll have to be quick, before
that ice tips them in the water.
I'll be back before you know it.
Just keep an eye on them."

Then Pat was gone, with Julian and Lucy huddled in the gateway, watching poor Katy and Tom wobbling out there on the ice.

Pat went as fast as he could, on the slippery road. He knew just where to go.

Ted Glen's workshop was not far away, and Ted had a long ladder. He also had a truck with a car phone in it. He was a useful man was Ted.

# Chapter Six

# Rescue!

Pat rushed into Ted's workshop
so fast that Ted spilt all his tea
on the carpet!

"Never mind that," shouted
Pat, "Katy and Tom are on the
ice, and it's cracking!"

Pat had never seen Ted move
so fast. He didn't know he
*could* move so fast!

Ted skimmed across the room,
and they were outside, with Ted
shouting, "Catch hold of that
ladder!" before Pat could get
his breath back.

They loaded the ladder on to
the truck, and were off down
the road, with Pat jabbing at
the buttons on Ted's phone, to
call the Greendale ambulance
and the police.

Julian and Lucy had seen them coming, and opened the gate, so Ted drove straight into the field, across the snow, to the edge of the water.

"Now, then," he said, "this is going to be a bit tricky, like, but I think we can do it."

Katy and Tom were still floating on their piece of ice, but it was wobbling more and more, and looked likely to tip them into that icy cold water any moment.

"Keep still!" shouted Ted.
"We're coming to get you!"
shouted Pat. "Don't be
frightened. You'll be all right."

Then he said to Julian and Lucy,
"Well done, you two. Now get
into the truck, and get nice
and warm."

They didn't need telling twice!
It was lovely in there, with the
heater going full blast.

## Chapter Seven

# The ice-ladder

What were Pat and Ted
doing with that ladder? It
seemed a funny thing to use
to rescue someone from the ice.
The ladder opened out like
a telescope.

It was really a lot of ladders joined together, so that Ted could slide it out, longer and longer, across the unsteady ice.

It made a kind of bridge over the ice.

Then Ted told Pat to creep
along this ladder-bridge,
slowly, slowly, towards
Katy and Tom.

The ladder would spread Pat's weight out, so the ice would not sink under him, and drop him into the cold water.

Well, that's what Ted hoped would happen. Ted had to kneel on the end of the ladder to hold it steady, and push Pat further and further out from the shore.

I don't know how they did it. It looked as if no one could do it. But, somehow, they did. Pat crept nearer and nearer.

The ice tipped and wobbled. Katy and Tom cried and hugged each other, and held their hands out to Pat.

Then there was a

# splash!

Their sledge slithered into the
water, and sank to the bottom.

At that moment, Pat caught
hold of the children, and
dragged them on to the ladder.

Ted pulled the ladder in to the
shore. They were wet and cold
and frightened but they were
safe, at last!

Pat and Katy and Tom
staggered across the snow.
Ted wrapped a big red blanket
round Katy and Tom, and
bundled them into the warm
truck.

# Chapter Eight

# A happy ending

It was then that the ambulance
and P.C. Selby's police car
came through the gate.

What a hugging and a kissing
Mrs Pottage gave Katy and
Tom when she came along!

And how pleased everyone
was with Julian and Lucy,
for getting help so quickly, to
rescue their friends on the ice.

"I'll tell you one thing," said
Pat, to them all. "We would all
have been in real trouble
without Ted's wonderful
ladders."
"And your wonderful van!"
said Ted, laughing.

When they got home, Katy
and Tom's mum gave them a
bowl of hot soup and a hot
bath.

At school, on Monday
morning, Mr Pringle said,
"Katy and Tom are lucky to be
alive. Lucy and Julian were
really sensible to get help so
quickly. Well done."

After that, every girl and boy
promised that they would *never
ever* play on the ice, or near the
ice, ever again.

"I'll help them to remember,"
said Ted. He painted a notice
in big red letters. It said:

Every winter, Ted puts this
notice up, by the lake. From
that day to this, no one ever
went on the ice again.

And a good thing too.